Figure 1

Turkmen boys at the archaeological site of Annau (date unknown; early 20th century).

TURKMENISTAN
ANCIENT ARTS TODAY

Figure 2

"The creators of Turkmen masterpieces,"
1984. A. Khadjiyev (1924-1998) Museum
of Fine Arts, Ashgabat.

Front cover, and title page (left to right):

The central rotunda of the Museum of Fine
Arts, Ashgabat, with equestrian sculpture
of Oguz Khan, legendary progenitor of
the Turkmen people, sculpted by Babayev
Saragt (1948-). (February 2011).

Detail of Floor Carpet , early 20th century,
Ahal region. Wool pile weaving with natural
dyes, 117 X 97 cm. Main National Museum
of Turkmenistan, Ashgabat, registry
number: Öws-579 "k." See Figure 26.

"Veterans," 1978. Kakamyrat Baýlyýew
(1949-1996). Gobelin, Wool and cotton flat
weaving, 220 X 180 cm. Museum of Fine
Arts, Ashgabat, registry number: AHS-1049
KEK-9843. See Figure 42.

Wedding (Toý), 1986, by Amanmyrat Ataýew
(1940-). Tempera painting with bronze inlay,
70 X 50 cm. Museum of Fine Arts, Ashgabat,
Registry number: Ž-527. See Figure 48.

Back cover (left to right):

▶ Detail of central panel, Prayer Rug.
  (Artist unknown, 2001). Wool pile
  weaving (120 X 80 cm). Museum of
  Fine Arts in Turkmenistan, registry
  number: PS-657. See Figure 39.

▶ The People's Orchestra of the National
  Conservatory performing In the
  Shade of the Happy Motherland! ("Şat
  Watanymyň saýasynda!") by Hydyr
  Allanurov, February 2011. Muhamed
  Gapurov (conductor/ faculty member)
  leads the orchestra at the National
  Conservatory; the portrait of
  Turkmenistan's President Gurbanguly
  Berdimuhamedov hangs above the
  stage.

▶ Exhibition of Turkmen textiles and
  crafts, Main National Museum of
  Turkmenistan (February 2011).

TURKMENISTAN
ANCIENT ARTS TODAY

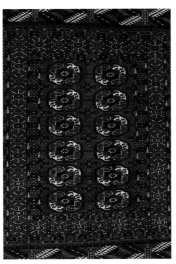

Paul Michael Taylor
Trevor Loomis Merrion
Jasper Waugh-Quasebarth
William Bradford Smith

Asian Cultural History Program | Smithsonian Institution | 2011

Published in conjunction with the **Turkmenistan Culture Days** in Washington, D.C. (November 28-30, 2011), held in recognition of Turkmenistan's twentieth anniversary of independence (1991-2011)

Events within the **Turkmenistan Culture Days** were co-organized by the Asian Cultural History Program (Smithsonian Institution), the U.S. Department of State, the Ministry of Culture of Turkmenistan, the U.S. Library of Congress, Meridian International Center, and other Washington-area institutions. Events include the Library of Congress-Smithsonian Symposium on the Literary and Performing Arts of Turkmenistan; the twentieth anniversary reception and the exhibition *Turkmenistan: Ancient Arts Today* at Meridian House (Meridian International Center), for which this publication also serves as catalog; and a concert at the Library of Congress's Coolidge Auditorium.

Artworks illustrated here were loaned for exhibition in Washington by the Main National Museum of Turkmenistan and the Museum of Fine Arts of Turkmenistan, and displayed at Meridian House as part of the **Turkmenistan Culture Days**.

This publication, and the cooperative work with Turkmenistan's museums that preceded it, have been made possible by generous support from Chevron.

Special thanks also to the U.S. Department of State, Embassy of the USA in Ashgabat, Turkmenistan.

ISBN: 978-0-9724557-8-7
First Edition

Cataloging-in-Publication Data

Turkmenistan : ancient arts today / Paul Michael Taylor, Trevor
   Loomis Merrion, Jasper Waugh-Quasebarth, William Bradford
   Smith. — 1st ed.
       p. cm.
   Includes bibliographical references.
   ISBN-13: 978-0-9724557-8-7
   1. Arts, Turkmen—Exhibitions. 2. Turkmen—Material
culture—Exhibitions. 3. Türkmenistan Milli Müzesi—
Exhibitions. 4. Türkmenistanyň Şekillendiriş Sungaty Muzeýi
—Exhibitions. I. Taylor, Paul Michael, 1953- II. Merrion,
Trevor Loomis, 1987- III. Waugh-Quasebarth, Jasper, 1990-
IV. Smith, William Bradford, 1984- V. National
Museum of Natural History (U.S.). Asian Cultural History Program.
VI. Meridian International Center (Washington, D.C.)
   NX575.7.T8 T87 2011

Figure 3

Turkmen women celebrate at the opening of a resort in Awaza on the Caspian Sea.

7

Figure 4

The capital city of Ashgabat has flourished since Turkmenistan declared its independence from the USSR in 1991.

Figure 5

Starkly beautiful desert landscapes
are common in the Kopet Dagh
mountain range that runs along the
southern border of Turkmenistan.

Figure 6
Professional weavers preserve and demonstrate traditional carpet-weaving methods at the Carpet Museum in Ashgabat.

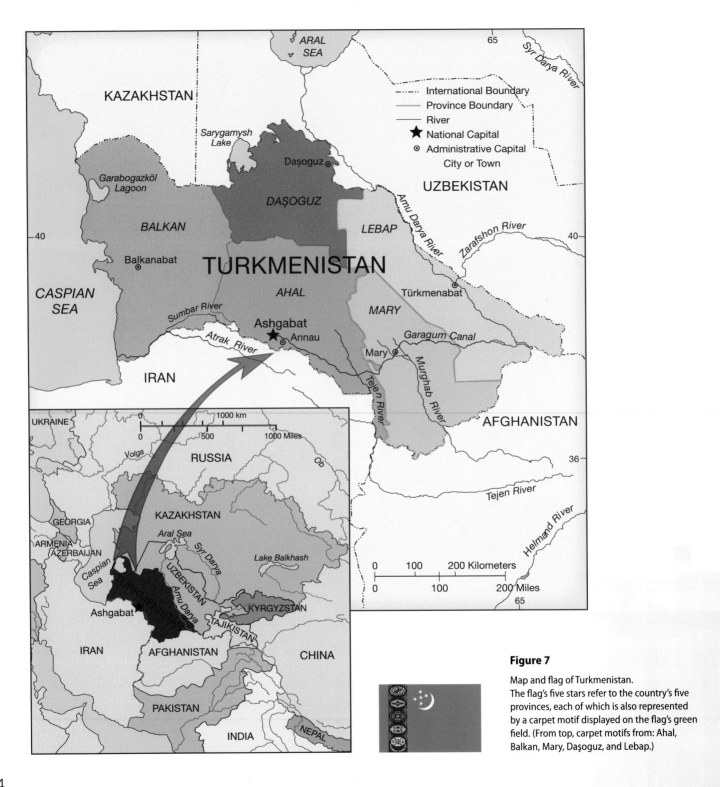

Figure 7

Map and flag of Turkmenistan.
The flag's five stars refer to the country's five provinces, each of which is also represented by a carpet motif displayed on the flag's green field. (From top, carpet motifs from: Ahal, Balkan, Mary, Daşoguz, and Lebap.)

Turkmenistan Today: The Past Inspires the Present

The 2011 celebration of Turkmenistan's twentieth anniversary of independence from the former Soviet Union has provided the fortuitous occasion for a series of events in Washington, D.C., including an unparalleled exhibition held at Meridian House (Meridian International Center) of examples of Turkmenistan's craft, textile, and art traditions. The authors of this publication have been fortunate to work with our colleagues at the Main National Museum and the Museum of Fine Arts (both in Ashgabat, Turkmenistan), and with the staff of Meridian International Center, to organize the exhibition and the series of activities known as **Turkmenistan Culture Days** in Washington, D.C. (November 28-30, 2011). The authors hope this publication will help to introduce Turkmenistan to a broad American public, and also serve as a record of the artworks displayed on the occasion of the November 2011 celebrations.

Figure 8

The Halkbank in Ashagabat features on its façade the national carpet pattern symbols representing the five welayats, or provinces, of Turkmenistan. These five carpet symbols are juxtaposed on Turkmenistan's national flag, and are also prominently used in architecture, advertising, book publishing, and other invocations of national unity.

Figure 9

The painting "Built by Turkmenbashi the Great" by A. Kuliyev (1966-) (with other artists), on display at the National Museum of Fine Arts in Ashgabat, celebrates the role of monumental architecture in the new vision of Ashgabat, and of Turkmenistan.

It seems especially appropriate, when celebrating an ancient land's recent independence, to reflect upon the nation's use and revival of ancient national symbols and forms. As we shall see, these forms are being revived and reinterpreted in unique and dynamic new ways to establish and celebrate a strong Turkmen national identity and unity in the twenty-first century. The examples illustrated in this brief introduction will hopefully hint at the strength, breadth and depth of Turkmenistan's efforts to rediscover, revive, and reinterpret icons and symbols drawn from the past history of the Turkmen people as they move into a globalized twenty-first century economic and international environment.

The activities of the Washington, DC., "Culture Days" take many forms, including a symposium at the Library of Congress on "The Literary and Performing Arts of Turkmenistan," master classes in Turkmen music at area universities, and a concert at the Coolidge Auditorium, in addition to the exhibition and independence events at Meridian House. For these events, over seventy participants constitute the Turkmenistan delegation, including Minister of Culture Gulmyrat Muradov, along with many performers, artists, museum experts, archeologists, and other cultural luminaries. Most of the American audiences will be seeing for the first time the range and quality of Turkmenistan's cultural productions.

American audiences will also surely witness, in various media — including literature, film, music, and visual arts — the extent to which Turkmenistan's dynamic artists today find inspiration in that country's past. Those who visit Turkmenistan will also recognize the highly public use and interpretation of the past, for example in monuments, museums, and the overall monumental architecture that has especially transformed Ashgabat in the last two decades.

Beyond the monuments of Ashgabat, foreigners who visit Turkmenistan will find a land area dominated by the Garagum desert, a region of a surpassing, nomadic beauty formed by flat, sandy desert fading into dunes then thrusting up into mountains in the southern part of the country. Turkmenistan is a part of Central Asia, in the area criss-crossed by Silk Road caravans, and now located between Russia, China, the Indian subcontinent and the Middle East. Situated in the southwest corner of this region, Turkmenistan shares borders with Iran and Afghanistan to the south and Kazakhstan and Uzbekistan to the north. The country is slightly larger than the state of California, with a total land mass of 188,445 square miles. The Caspian Sea to the west provides Turkmenistan with significant natural gas and petroleum reserves as well as the means to a substantial import and export industry. The Amu Darya, known as the Oxus River in antiquity, is sourced by the glacial waters of Tian Shan and the Pamir Mountains in the south and flows through eastern Turkmenistan, providing water to the capital of Ashgabat via the Garagum Canal. The predominantly Sunni Muslim population is largely ethnically Turkmen but with minorities of ethnic Uzbeks, Russians, and others. About one fifth of the country's five million people live in or around Ashgabat, making it the largest city in the country, above the other principal cities of Mary, Türkmenbaşy, Turkmenabat and Daşoguz.

The country is dotted with archeological remains of the cities and caravan routes of the past. Since independence, there has been substantial growth in the establishment of historic and cultural preserves, and the development of archeological research and presentation at major monumental sites such as the ancient city of Merv. Certainly these sites have as their primary purpose the discovery and interpretation of Turkmenistan's past; the finds and data they produce are also sent to the rapidly growing national museum system.

Figure 10

The People's Orchestra of the National Conservatory performing *In the Shade of the Happy Motherland! ("Şat Watanymyň saýasynda!")* by Hydyr Allanurov, February 2011. Muhamed Gapurov (conductor/faculty member) leads the orchestra at the National Conservatory; the portrait of Turkmenistan's President Gurbanguly Berdimuhamedov hangs above the stage.

Figure 11

A traditional yurt surrounded by handmade carpets is prominently displayed within the marble setting of the National Carpet Museum in Ashgabat.

Clearly, museums and cultural institutions are flourishing in Turkmenistan, as attested by the rapid growth of cultural monuments in Ashgabat, including the Main National Museum complex (first opened in 1998), the Museum of Fine Arts (opened in 2005), and many other museums such as the renowned Carpet Museum (opened in 1993). There are also new provincial museums in each of the regional capitals, and many special site museums. These museums stand alongside other important cultural centers such as the country's music Conservatory (reorganized from the former State Pedagogical Institute of Arts and reopened in 1992 as the Turkmen National Conservatory). All these organizations have witnessed major growth in recent years (see TMTM 2009), and they have the potential to provide numerous benefits, such as a greater role for museums in the education of Turkmen of all ages, better local and international exposure of craft industries that already constitute important exports, and increased domestic and international tourism.

Turkmenistan's centrality in the history of Central Asia (such as the historic role of Merv as a center of learning and one of the world's most populous cities prior to its destruction during the 13th century Mongol invasions), and the authenticity and historic depth of its music or its craft and textile traditions (rich with symbolism and continuing strong today), are inadequately known outside Turkmenistan. We are grateful that cooperative exhibitions such as this one hosted by Meridian House, especially alongside other cultural exchanges taking place during Washington's Turkmenistan Culture Days, will surely increase awareness of Turkmenistan's unique and extensive efforts to find vision and inspiration for this new country's direction from the rich heritage of its own past.

History

The region included within
modern-day Turkmenistan has
been inhabited since at least
the 7th millennium BC, as cave
dwellings on the Caspian Sea
indicate early human presence
dating to that period (Frumkin
1970:129). Crop raising cultures
developed in the subsequent
millennia, and by 5000 BC,
nascent agricultural settlements
were common in the region. For
example, the archaeological site
of Dzheytun, about 30 km outside
of contemporary Ashgabat, is
one of the earliest examples of
a farming community in Central
Asia (Frumkin 1970:130).

Figure 12

A Turkmen man poses in the
ruins of the ancient city of
Merv, an important trade
hub on the Great Silk Road
(Date unknown, early 20th
century).

Figure 13

The ruins of the Khwarezm mosque and minaret at the ancient city of Köneürgenç serve as reminders of the rich cultural history of Turkmenistan.

By the 4th millennium BC this farming culture had spread east into the Margiana Oasis, sustained by the Amu Darya River, leading to the establishment of larger settlements in the Kopetdagh Piedmont (Frumkin 1970:130). This collection of related, late Bronze Age sites and settlements, including the archaeological sites of Altyn-Depe, Namazga-Depe and Gonur-Depe, dominated the region from around 2300 BC until 1700 BC and is commonly referred to as the Bactria-Margiana Archaeological Complex. This culture is noted for its extensive craft achievements, such as hand-built pottery, jewelry and golden sculptures of bull and wolf heads found at Altyn-Depe (Frumkin 1970:138; Masson 1988:3). Archaeological evidence also suggests contact and trade with Mesopotamia, Iran and India which may have been this culture's most lasting legacy (Frumkin 1970:138).

By the 4th century BC, nomadic Scythian tribes from north of the Caspian Sea had co-opted these regional connections into the more cohesive political structure of one of the first Central Asian empires. Through the exploitation of trade connections with the surrounding culturally diverse groups, the Scythians fashioned extensive networks of exchange between eastern and western markets (Beckwith 2009:59).

These developing trade routes attracted empire builders eager to increase their economic capacity, and by 500 BC the area was under the influence of the Achaemenid Persian Empire in the form of several tributary provinces. In 330 BC, Alexander the Great toppled the Achaemenids and took control of cities in Margiana that would become crucial hubs of trade, such as the city of Merv on the Murgab River. Despite the collapse of the Macedonian empire shortly after Alexander's death in 323 BC, the area remained deeply connected to the Hellenistic world through the Seleucids, decedents of the Macedonians, and their successors. The Seleucid Empire ruled for a short period before Iranian tribes seized power and laid the foundation for what would become the Parthian Empire, ruling from the city of Nisa (Frumkin 1970:142). While Nisa had been an active center of trade since the 6th century BC, it was during Parthian rule that it reached its zenith. Characterized by its Greek and Persian style art and architecture, especially ornate, ivory rhytons, Nisa embodied the Hellenistic and Persian cultural infusion in Central Asia and is an example of the continued importance of cultural diversity to the area (Frumkin 197veri0:145).

Arab invasions in the mid-7th century AD introduced Islam and brought significant societal transformations to the region (Brown 1849). The area supported some of the most respected centers of commerce and scholarship in the world, encouraging further exchange and trade in Central Asia (Starr 2009:36). The ancient cities of Merv, Köneürgenç on the Amu Darya River and Annau near the Kopet Dagh Mountains were centers of Muslim knowledge and scholarship and home to famed intellectuals such as Abu al-Rayhan al-Biruni (973- 1048) and Abu Ali Sina (c. 980-1037) who wrote extensively on the topics of medicine, mathematics, natural science, history and philosophy (Starr 2009:33). Architecture also reached new heights, as mosques and minarets were built that rivaled those in other parts of the Muslim world. For example, the Gutluk-Temir minaret in Köneürgenç was known to be one of the most impressive in the Muslim world. Trade networks between east and west continued to flourish under caliphate and sultanate rule, as Merv and the other urban centers became essential components of the Great Silk Road. By connecting Central Asian traders to the markets of the Muslim dynasties and beyond, these cities were instrumental in the transmission of commodities such as silk, wool, spices, carpets and precious metals across the medieval world (Christian 2000:8, Abazov 2005:71).

By the early 13th century, the Khwarezmids, a Turkic, Muslim sultanate, ruled all of what is now Turkmenistan from the city of Köneürgenç. To the east, Genghis Khan was expanding the Mongol Empire into one of the world's largest and sought to foster better trade relations on the Silk Road between his empire and the sultanate. However, upon hearing that his trade emissaries had been abused and humiliated by a local governor, the Khan immediately ordered a campaign to capture and destroy the Khwarezm cities. After sacking Samarkand and Bukhara in what is now Uzbekistan, the Mongols turned their destructive gaze to Köneürgenç and completely destroyed the city in one of the bloodiest massacres in human history. After the destruction of the northern cities, the Mongols looked south to Merv and the greater Khorosan province. In 1221, the Mongol army besieged Merv and subjected it to the same devastation and massacre as the other Khwarezm cities. Despite the extent of such ruthless destruction, cities such as Merv and Köneürgenç recovered slowly, bearing witness to the fracture of the Mongol Empire in the 14th century.

Figure 14

A Turkmen man stands among the ruins of the ancient city of Annau (Date unknown, early 20th century).

However, at end of the century, the Timurid dynasty, seeking to reclaim Mongol grandeur, all but completely destroyed the cities and left the once significant trading centers in ruins among the drifting sands.

It is indicative of the resilience of the Turkmen people that they are one of the earliest known Turkic groups in Central Asia, with a history that predates the Mongol invasions (Krader 1963:68). This history began sometime between the 8th and 11th centuries when Oguz Turks migrating west from Inner Asia encountered Muslim settlers on the Persian frontier and converted to Islam (Saray 1989:1). When Seljuk ibn Dudak split from the Oguz Turks in the 11th century, some Turkmen supported him in his campaign to establish the Seljuk dynasty and migrated beyond Central Asia. Meanwhile, the remaining Turkmen endured the Mongol invasion and settled in the Balkan Mountains, the Mangyshlak Peninsula and the Atrak steppes in what is today western Turkmenistan (Żerańska-Kominek 1997:22-23).

Figure 15

Since ancient times, Turkmen have recognized Oguz Khan as the progenitor of the Turkmen people. Today, artists often evoke his image, honoring him as a national hero.

Figure 16

Turkmen women outside a yurt, the
Turkmen traditional nomadic dwelling
(Date unknown, early 20th century)
(From print: In Captivity and Turkmen
Khivans, Moscow, 1914).

Though there are earlier historical accounts of the
Turkmen, Persian historian Rashid al-Din's chronicle
from the 14th century, *Djame al-Tavarikh*, is notable
for its reference to the Oguz Khan narrative,
which contains an explanation of the origin of
the Turkmen people (Azadi 1975:6). According to
this narrative, the Oguz Turkic warrior-hero Oguz
Khan had twenty-four grandsons, who each went
on to found a tribe in what would later be known
as the Oguz Federation (Schletzer 1984:15-16).
To this day the Turkmen recognize Oguz Khan
as their legendary progenitor. Though primarily
based on oral histories and folk legend, several of
the tribes mentioned in al-Din's early chronicle,
such as the Salyr and Chovdur, were still present in
Turkmenistan into the 19th century (Azadi 1975:7).

As the Turkmen resettled in the 14th and 15th centuries after over two hundred years of warfare, a tribal confederation developed behind the leadership of the Salyr. This alliance of tribes, which included the Salyr, Tekke, Saryk, Yomud and Ersari, comprised the majority of tribes that would rise to prominence in the next five hundred years of Turkmen history. This alliance began to disintegrate in the 17th century, largely due to limited access to fresh water and warfare with neighboring states. For the nomadic Turkmen, who tended large herds, healthy pasture required reliable water resources. As the Saragamysh Lake and lower Amu Darya River gradually dried, the Ersari migrated southeast towards the middle Amu Darya, while the Salyr, Saryk and Tekke settled in the oases of the Murghab delta (Tsareva 2011:17; Schletzer 1984:17-18). The Yomud remained predominantly in the Balkan Mountains, but settled as far northeast as the region between the Aral Sea and Khiva. Meanwhile, the Chovdur had formed their own alliance in the north. Tribal distribution therefore approximated modern borders with the Tekke in Ahal, the Yomud in Balkan, the Chovdur in Daşoguz, the Ersari in Lebap and the Salyr and Saryk in Mary.

The other major determinant of settlement patterns was the persistent incursion of the Bukhara Emirate, Khiva Khanate and Persian state into Turkmen territory between the 17th and 19th centuries (Abazov 2005:lvii). By the late 19th century, certain Turkmen tribes had become subjects of these state powers, particularly the Yomuds in Khiva and the Ersari in Bukhara (Edgar 2004:27). While they paid a tribute at times, it is important to remember that due to the mobility and military prowess of the Turkmen, this subjugation was often merely nominal and limited in its imposition upon the Turkmen (Edgar 2004:27; Irons 1975:7). Many Turkmen in the late 19th century continued to live as pastoral nomads and maintained large flocks of sheep, goats and camels. Others developed a more sedentary existence based around subsistence farming, while a few small communities of Turkmen craftsmen and weavers produced goods for sale and exchange in bazaars (Abazov 2005:lix). Regardless of occupation, the Turkmen continued to live in yurts like their ancestors, to marry according to traditional customs and to settle disputes in adherence to the unwritten common law of the Turkmen, known as *adat* (Blackwell 2001:38; Edgar 2003).

Figure 17

Turkmen men of the Tekke tribe in Southern Turkmenistan (Date unknown, early 20th century). (From: Semenov-Tian-Shanskii, Veniamin Petrovich, Russia: A Complete Geographical Survey of Our Nation, St. Petersburg: 1914).

As Russian interests extended into lower Central Asia in the late 19th century, the benefits of their form of modernity were accompanied by the costs of occupation. The Turkmen were relieved of threats from Bukhara in 1868 and Khiva in 1873, when the Russians conquered these sovereignties and held them as protectorates. However, this reprieve was short-lived as the Turkmen were forced to defend themselves against a Russian advance only a few years later. In 1892, Russia established the Zacaspian *oblast* (province) and the Turkmen way of life rapidly began to transform. The construction of the Zacaspian railroad in the 1880s introduced many foreign goods to the region, such as steel and glassware, but it also encouraged subsistence agriculturists to begin growing cash crops such as cotton, which significantly altered the Turkmen economy (Abazov 2005:lix-lx). The Russians also introduced education in the form of so-called native schools, but these were reserved for an elite few who were groomed to maintain the colonial administration. These factors, along with the influx of Russians and other foreigners

Figure 18

"Century Dream Is Fulfilled," 1962. A. Khadjiyev (1924-1998), Museum of Fine Arts, Ashgabat.

who were eager to capitalize on trade and political opportunities, created new social dynamics that had not existed before among the Turkmen. Though the Russian occupation of Central Asia brought a degree of peace to a historically war-wrought region, it was to the detriment of the Turkmen traditional culture and independence.

Figure 19

The Independence Monument in Ashgabat was erected to commemorate the establishment of an independent Turkmenistan on October 27, 1991.

This tenuous peace was broken in 1916 when the Turkmen initiated major uprisings in response to the Tsar's decree to enlist thousands of Turkmen for the Russian war effort. The violence continued until the end of the decade, as the Bolshevik Revolution of 1917 led to a Russian civil war that spread throughout Central Asia and lasted until 1920. Warfare, coupled with several years of famine, resulted in a twenty-five percent decline in Turkmen population between 1915 and 1920 (Edgar 2004:37). As the Bolsheviks stabilized power in the 1920s and developed nationality policies to foster unity among the vast number of ethnicities in Central Asia, there was hope for an independent and autonomous Turkmen state. In 1924, the Soviets demarcated Central Asia along ethnic boundaries and the Turkmen Soviet Socialist Republic was formed. However, establishing national borders did little to improve the political authority of the Turkmen. Ultimately, the implementation of unwanted collectivization policies, purges of the Turkmen intelligentsia, perpetuation of a nepotistic political system and limited regard for Turkmen common law and customs undermined Soviet attempts to foster an autonomous Turkmenistan (Abazov 2005:lxxxvii-lxxxviii).

On October 27, 1991, the government of Turkmenistan declared its independence from the Union of Soviet Socialist Republics. After over a century of foreign interference, the social and cultural milieu in Turkmenistan had changed significantly. In this post-independence time of revival, the traditional culture that persisted for many centuries before has become the focal point for a newly independent and unified Turkmenistan.

Music

The Music of Turkmenistan represents an ancient art form that maintains both traditional practice and a relevance to modern culture. Among the earliest historical records of the Turkmen professional oral epic singers, the *bagshy*, are the epic poem *Korut Ata* (or *Dede Korut*) which is dated to the 6th or 7th century A.D. (Kurbanova 2000 : 118) The Hero of this poem, named Korkut, is a singer (*ozan*) who assembles oral epics of the Oghuz which later became popular in the singing tradition of the Turkmen people. The *bagshy* in modern Turkmenistan are considered elite vocalists and *dutar* practitioners capable of memorizing massive amounts of music and epic poetry, who exhibit improvisational techniques specific to their region.

Figure 20

The instruments commonly used in Turkmen traditional music. Clockwise from left: the *garghy tüydük* (flute), the *ghidjak* and two examples of the *dutar*.

Prospective Turkmen *bagshy* are required to study for several years under a master (*Khalypa*) before receiving the *pata* of his teacher (from the Arabic fatiha "blessing") and earning the title of *bagshy*. (Kurbanova 2000 : 116)

The *dutar* serves as the primary accompaniment for the *bagshy* and is the principal instrument in Turkmen traditional music. The word *dutar* derives from the Persian words "du" meaning two and "tar" meaning string. The *dutar* is a two-string fretted lute tuned to the interval of a fourth which is constructed in four segments. The sections of the *dutar* include the *kadi* (resonator), *gapak* (soundboard), *sap* (neck) and the *eshek* (bridge). The *dutar* is mostly constructed from Turkmen Apricot, Mulberry, and Walnut wood, as well as steel for the frets, strings, and tuners. (Fossum 2010: 40) Older variations of frets and strings were made from silk which resulted in historic differences in the tone and resonance of the instrument. Steel strings and frets were introduced around the 1930's and were widely accepted amongst musicians as an improvement to silk due to the enrichment in tonality and increased dynamic capability. (Fossum 2010: p. 44)

Figure 22

At the National Conservatory in Ashgabat, students master a variety of Central Asian instruments, including the Turkmen *dutar* and *ghidjak*.

The construction process of the *dutar* begins by baking the mulberry wood for the *gapak* (soundboard) in a clay oven to soften the wood. The wood is positioned vertically inside the oven to create an uneven bake that allows the wood nearer to the *sap* (neck) to retain its hardness and withstand the strumming of the dutarist's hand over many years. The *gapak* is then glued to the *kadi* and punctured with small holes in an arranged pattern specific to the artisan as a form of maker's mark. (Fossum 2010: 41)

Figure 23

At the National Conservatory, Turkmen students often play traditional songs in groups comprised solely of Turkmen instruments.

Other traditional Turkmen instruments include the *ghidjak*, a bowed two-string fiddle, the *garghy tüydük*, a long end-blown flute, and the *dilli tüydük*, a smaller shepherd's pipe. A practitioner of the *ghidjak*, known as a *gidzhakchi*, may accompany the *bagshy* in the northern Tashauz (Dashoguz) performance style. *Bagshy* singers are likely to pick a compatible *gidzhakchi* early in their musical career and continue to collaborate with same musician for a lifetime. (Kurbanova 2000: 122)

The *bagshy* may be categorized into two types: the *bagshy tirmechi* and the *bagshy dessanchi*. The *bagshy tirmechi* perform songs featuring lyrics based on works of the classical native poets of Turkmenistan, and exhibit an extraordinary memory to assist in playing functions such as a feast (*toý*) which often will require the *bagshy* to perform for many hours. The *bagshy dessanchi* perform songs from lengthy oral epics called *dessans*. *Dessans* were mostly composed by other *bagshy* or poets would often choose to remain anonymous as composers. The *dessan* requires intense concentration and memorization as some of the oral epics can last up to twenty-four hours and require the *bagshy* to split the work into as many as seven separate sections. Turkmen ethnomusicologist Djamilya Kurbanova writes of the *Dessanchi*, "The *bagshy* does not simply re-tell the *dessan*, but he also re-creates it." (*ibid.*, p. 121)

The *bagshy* utilize many vocal and instrumental techniques to achieve the musical journey of a *dessan*. Distinctive features to note when listening to a *bagshy* include the ornamentation and the "sound effects" performed between the stanzas of lyrics. There are three major vocal techniques used to increase intensity and overall experience of a performance: the *djukguldamak*, the *khulemek*, and the *khumlemek*. These vocal sound effects serve to distinguish an individual *bagshy*'s musical style and to identify the region from which the singer originated. The *djukguldamak* or "*djuk-djuk*" is a vocalization produced with a succession of glottal stops using the vocal cord on the vowels "i," or "a," depending on the performance school of the *bagshy*. The *khulemek* is characterized by a reduction of a single syllable "*khu*" to a low register of the singer's voice and often has an indefinite pitch. The singer may also demonstrate a variation of the *khulemek* technique in which the mouth is closed, known as "*khumlemek*." In addition to these vocal techniques, *bagshy* will employ a variety of ornamentations on exclamations such as "*kha*," "*khe*," "*ey*," etc. The exclamation allows the *bagshy* to develop a performance atmosphere and is intended to capture the listener's attention. (Zeranska-Kominek 1990: 96)

Modern Turkmenistan holds an active interest in the preservation and pedagogy of musical forms and instrument craftsmanship. The Turkmen National Conservatory was established in the capital of Ashgabat in 1992 as a revitalization of the Turkmen State Pedagogical Institute of Arts which was established under Soviet rule in 1972 (TNC n.d.:[1]). Today's active Conservatory testifies to the dedication of the Turkmen people in ensuring a future for ancient and modern musical forms. The National Conservatory also offers courses in the performance of instruments from around the world, and features a variety of ensembles from the symphonic orchestra to the smaller folk ensembles and *bagshy* masters.

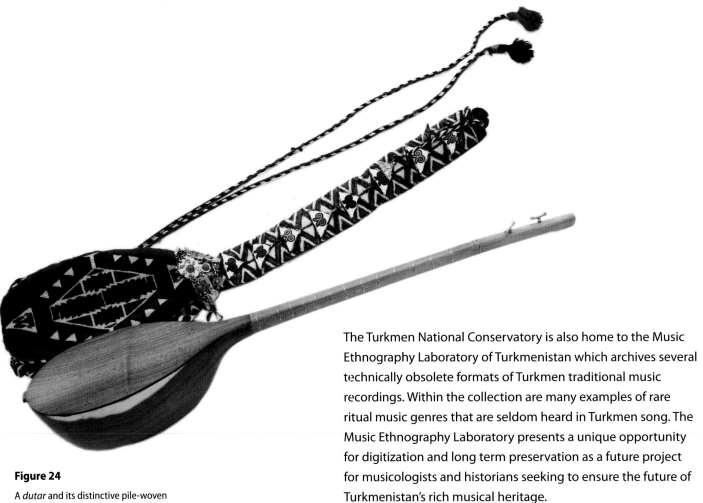

The Turkmen National Conservatory is also home to the Music Ethnography Laboratory of Turkmenistan which archives several technically obsolete formats of Turkmen traditional music recordings. Within the collection are many examples of rare ritual music genres that are seldom heard in Turkmen song. The Music Ethnography Laboratory presents a unique opportunity for digitization and long term preservation as a future project for musicologists and historians seeking to ensure the future of Turkmenistan's rich musical heritage.

Figure 24

A *dutar* and its distinctive pile-woven carrying bag, featuring motifs present in other carpet products.

Exhibited Works

In this section, we offer a basic description of the works displayed at Meridian House in Washington during the events of Turkmenistan Culture Days 2011. These objects have been generously loaned for this occasion by Turkmenistan's Ministry of Culture and are drawn from the collections of the Main National Museum and Museum of Fine Arts in Ashgabat.

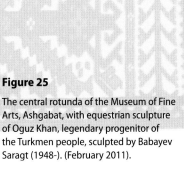

Figure 25

The central rotunda of the Museum of Fine Arts, Ashgabat, with equestrian sculpture of Oguz Khan, legendary progenitor of the Turkmen people, sculpted by Babayev Saragt (1948-). (February 2011).

Traditional Turkmen carpets are characterized by the ubiquitous use of red dyes and by the *göl*, an emblematic design repeated in the central field of the carpet. This iconic style is applied across a range of carpet products from conventional rugs to storage bags. Specific variations on the *göl* motif are associated with particular Turkmen tribes, allowing one to identify the provenance of a carpet based on design. With the location of Turkmen tribes relatively established by the early 19th century, the regional provenance of most Turkmen rugs also may be determined by the *göl* motif. Though several economic and political factors have undermined the connection between *göl* and identity in the 20th century, this connection is nonetheless preserved today on the national flag, where the five *göls* featured represent the five provinces of Turkmenistan.

Figure 26

Floor Carpet

Ahal region

Early 20th century

Wool, pile weaving with natural dyes

117 X 97 cm

Main National Museum (Ashgabat)

Registry number: Öws-579 "k"

The floor carpets seen here, known as *halis*, are the largest type of carpet produced by Turkmen weavers. Traditionally, Turkmen would lay the *hali* inside their yurt, a portable dwelling made of wood and felt, to welcome guests and family members. Upon entering, one would know the tribal affiliation of the host by the *göl* in the center field of their *hali* (Azadi 1975:19).

These two Ahal *halis* (Figure 26 and Figure 27) can be associated with the Tekke of Ahal because they feature a specific *gol*, the *gushly gol* (Figure 28). Though the Tekke are known to use other *göls*, the *gushly göl* is used so frequently it is often also referred to as the Tekke *göl*. Translated as "bird's lake" *göl*, the three-prong designs repeated in each quadrant of the medallion are intended to represent bird's feet. The use of established designs such as the *gushly göl* allows weavers to produce carpets efficiently. However, as carpets are traditionally woven from memory a degree of variation is inevitable, illustrated by these two Ahal carpets.

Figure 27

Floor Carpet
Ahal region
Late 19th to early 20th century
Wool, pile weaving with natural dyes
181 X 128 cm
Main National Museum (Ashgabat)
Registry number: Öws – 616

Figure 28

The *gushly göl* pattern of the Ahal-Tekke is the preeminent carpet design in Turkmenistan and is the only *göl* featured on the famous "Golden Age" carpet, one of the largest handmade carpets in the world.

The Balkan *hali* (Figure 29) is distinguished by the *gabsa göl* of the Yomud, who have historically occupied the Balkan region. The *gabsa göl*, interpreted as a birdcage, is characterized by its diamond shape and bars of alternating color. (Moshkova et al. 1996: 236). There is no apparent difference between this 21st century *gabsa göl* and those from the 19th century, exemplifying the resiliency of Turkmen carpet designs. Technique also was preserved through the use of natural dyes, indicating that the trend towards synthetic dyes in the 20th century has not entirely supplanted traditional dyeing methods.

Figure 29

Floor Carpet

Balkan region

Early 21st century

Wool, pile weaving with natural dyes

207 X 126 cm

Main National Museum (Ashgabat)

Registry number: KEK-3933

Named for the Pendi Oasis in the Mary region, the *pendi göl* on the Mary *hali* (Figure 30) was traditionally associated with the Salyr, as this tribe was the first to settle in the region and utilize the pattern. However, the pattern was borrowed with slight variations by the Saryk and Tekke to meet consumer demand for the design in the late 19th and early 20th centuries (Moshkova et al. 1996: 179). When a *göl* is known to have been appropriated by other tribes, carpet experts must rely on technical features, such as knot technique, to determine a carpet's provenance (Baýryýewa 2008, 23). In this case, the carpet has been identified by experts at the Main National Museum of Turkmenistan as a Salyr weaving.

Figure 30
Floor Carpet
Mary region
Early 20th century
Wool, pile weaving with natural dyes
181 X 135 cm
Main National Museum (Ashgabat)
Registry number: KEK-4369 Öws-744 "k"

Figure 31

Saddle Bag
Mary region
Early 20th century
Wool, pile weaving with natural dyes
52 X 93 cm
Main National Museum (Ashgabat)
Registry number: KEK-667 "h"

Turkmen weaving is not limited to conventional floor carpets. As wool was one of the only surplus materials available to Turkmen sheep herding communities, weavers fashioned numerous wool products that complemented the nomadic way of life. Consequently, a Turkmen possessed many products made of wool, from a variety of bags to the roof they slept under. Despite the utilitarian purpose of many of these products, they were often decorated as lavishly as prominent floor carpets.

Double-sided saddle bags known as a *khorjuns* (Figure 31) were aptly suited for the nomadic lifestyle of the Turkmen. Since they did not typically come much larger than the example shown here, they also could be worn over the shoulder when traveling. By the late 19th century, many smaller carpet items such as the *khorjun* were produced primarily for the market (Moshkova et al. 1996: 53). Though typically serving a strictly utilitarian purpose, brides on their wedding day also may receive a *khorjun* filled with sweets to take with them in celebration of their nuptials.

Larger carpet bags, known as *chuvals* (Figure 32) were used by all Turkmen tribes. They are typically woven as a pair so that they may easily hang from the sides of a horse or camel when in transit, much like the *khorjun*. This particular example of a *chuval* is designated as a *chuval yuzi*, meaning "bag face," implying that this is only the front decorative panel of the bag. When not traveling, the Turkmen would hang the *chuvals* from the inner walls of the yurt to provide storage for household items.

Figure 32
Carpet Bag
Mary region
Late 19th century
Wool, pile weaving with natural dyes
91 X 167 cm
Main National Museum (Ashgabat)
Registry number: KEK-2454 Öws-562 "k"

Turkmen carpets traditionally include one or more horizontal borders known as the älem. This design feature is unique to Turkmen weaving and may be found either on the top or bottom of the carpet (Stone 2007: 277). This *chuval* (Figure 33) is referred to as an *ak chuval*, or "white bag," because of its distinctive white älem. The pattern within this älem is a repetition of the "tree of life" motif, which is believed to promote health and prosperity. Variations on the "tree of life" motif occur frequently in Turkmen carpets and textiles.

The yurt decoration (Figure 34) also features a similar white älem with the repeating "tree of life" pattern. This carpet is known as an ümür *duman*, or "fog carpet," because it is hung from the upper corners of the yurt ceiling, imitating fog in the sky. Unlike most Turkmen carpet products, the ümür *duman* is strictly for decorative purposes. The main design in the ümür *duman* is not considered a *göl* but rather a spiraled variation on the common *gochak* motif (Figure 35). The *gochak* represents ram's horns and is believed to provide protective powers (Figure 36).

Figure 33

Carpet Bag
Ahal or Balkan region
Late 19th century to early 20th century
Wool, flat weaving with natural dyes
143 X 78 cm
Main National Museum (Ashgabat)
Registry number: KEK-946/1 Öws-598/1 "k"

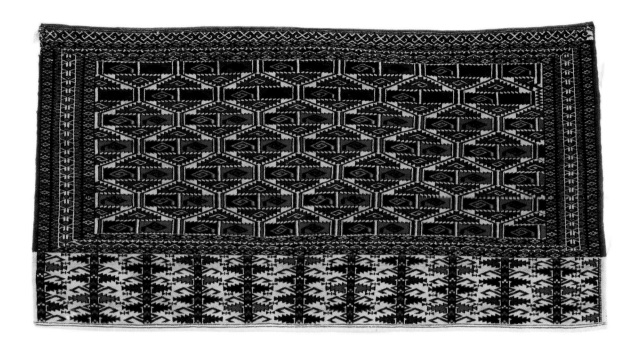

Figure 34

Yurt Decoration
Ahal region
Late 19th century
Wool, pile with natural dyes
62 X 117 cm
Main National Museum (Ashgabat)
Registry number: KEK-35 ÖWS-373 "h"

Figure 35

The spirals in this design are considered variations on the *gochak* motif.

Figure 36

The white extensions resembling ram's horns on this *göl* are examples of the standard *gochak* motif.

Figure 37

Camel Adornment

All regions of Turkmenistan

Late 19th century to early 20th century

Silk and cotton, cloth stitching

94 X 126 cm

Main National Museum (Ashgabat)

Registry number: Öws-64/3 "m.ö."

These camel adornments (Figure 37 and Figure 38), known as a *gapylyk* or *khalyk*, are used primarily as a decoration for the lead camel during a bridal procession. It is worn on the front of the camel so that the extensions of the *gapylyk* adorn the camel's legs. After the procession, the *gapylyk*, which translates to "for door," is hung over the opening to the newlyweds' yurt so the groom may flaunt his wife's skill as a weaver (Tsareva 1984, 9).

While most traditional *gapylyk* are pile woven, this checkered *gapylyk* (Figure 37) is fashioned by stitching small pieces of fabric together. The technique is known as *gurama* and is commonly used when producing everyday, household goods.

The modern *gapylyk*, "New Revival" (Figure 38) by Amanmyrat Ataýew, applies neither the *gurama* nor the pile-weaving technique, but rather a flat weaving technique commonly used by modern artists. This piece illustrates the presence of traditional forms in modern Turkmen art, as the artist utilizes non-traditional weaving techniques to replicate a past aesthetic.

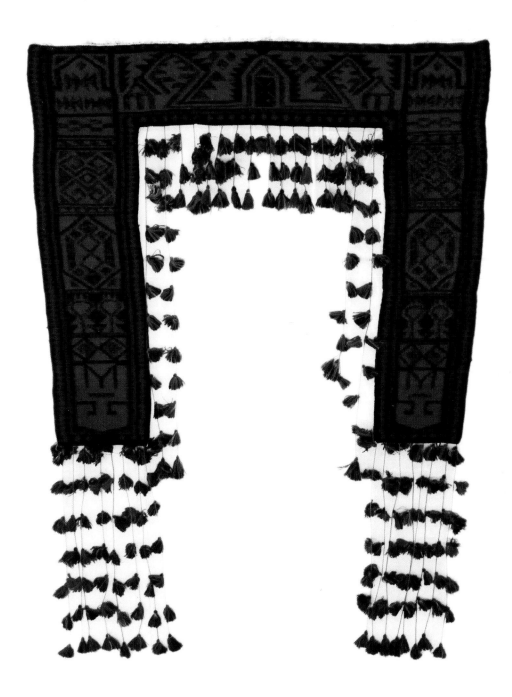

Figure 38
"New Revival" ("*Galkynma*")
Amanmyrat Ataýew (1940-)
20th century
Wool, flat weaving
181 X 192 cm
Museum of Fine Arts (Ashgabat)
Registry number: AHS-140

Several other items on exhibit also exemplify the synthesis between traditional form and modern content. The prayer rug (Figure 39) or *namazlyk*, is woven in the traditional *ensi* style and is rich with Islamic imagery including representations of the *mihrab*, or prayer niche, and a mosque. The inscription along the top border honoring Turkmenbashi, or former president Saparmyrat Niyazov, is a modern element not featured in these rugs traditionally.

The carpet portrait of Magtymguly (Figure 40), a famous poet and national hero of Turkmenistan, is another modern adaptation of the traditional aesthetic. With the development of synthetic dyes in the 20th century, the color palette available to weavers expanded, enabling experimentation beyond the traditional geometric patterns. Many began weaving carpets containing more realist images, while still incorporating traditional patterns in the borders and älem. The effect this juxtaposition creates is that of the past framing the present, an aesthetic permeating Turkmen culture today.

Figure 39

Prayer Rug

Artist unknown

2002

Wool, pile weaving

120 X 80 cm

Museum of Fine Arts (Ashgabat)

Registry number: PS-657

Figure 40

Carpet Portrait of Magtymguly

Artist unknown

Mid-20th century

Wool and cotton, pile weaving

142 X 91 cm

Museum of Fine Arts (Ashgabat)

Registry number: K-579 KEK-5984

Figure 41

Carpet

Artist unknown

Late 20th to early 21st century

Wool, pile weaving

97 X 74 cm

Museum of Fine Arts (Ashgabat)

Registry number: PS-456

The traditional jewelry worn by Turkmen women was the basis for many carpet designs. For example, the 16-pointed star design used for the main border of the Tekke *hali* (Figure 26) is a representation of pectoral jewelry worn by Turkmen women. In the "brooch" carpet (Figure 41), the source for inspiration is the šelpeli *gulyaka*, an item of pectoral jewelry common in all regions of Turkmenistan (Schletzer et al. 1984: 200-201). The combination of this image with traditional motifs, such as the *gushly göl*, makes this carpet a compelling example of the crossover between traditional and modern designs.

Many modern Turkmen carpets do not contain any traditional design elements. Known as gobelins, they are specifically works by artists trained in the French weaving style at Soviet art schools. They are related in technique to traditional Turkmen flat weavings, or *kilims*, but because they were often woven by men and viewed strictly as works of art, the gobelins represent a departure from tradition. Nonetheless, continuity between traditional carpets and gobelins is fostered through the reiteration of themes often found in traditional carpets, such as nature and Turkmen culture. The gobelin shown here by Kakamyrat Baýlyýew, titled "Veterans" (Figure 42) depicts two Turkmen elders in traditional sheepskin hats as they prepare tea over an open fire.

Figure 42

"Veterans" ("*Weteranlar*")

Kakamyrat Baýlyýew (1949-1996)

1978

Wool and cotton, gobelin flat weaving

220 X 180 cm

Museum of Fine Arts (Ashgabat)

Registry number: AHS-1049 KEK-9843

The gobelin "Charva Turkmens" (Figure 43) by Annaguly Hojagulyýew is comprised of scenes from nature and the nomadic life as images of camels, a gazelle and a wolf are interspersed with a Turkmen woman and a hunter drawing his bow. *Charva* refers to the Turkmen that maintained the ideal of the nomadic lifestyle into the 19th century. These Turkmen were distinguished from the relatively sedentary *chomur* who had to rely on subsistence agriculture for their livelihood.

Figure 43

"Charva Turkmens" (*"Çarwa türkmenleri"*)

Annaguly Hojagulyýew (1947-)

20th century

Wool and cotton, gobelin flat weaving

66 X 87 cm

Museum of Fine Arts (Ashgabat)

Registry number: R-38 KEK-2336 (124 nf)

"Our Home" (Figure 44) by Annaguly Hojagulyýew and Sulgun Hojagulyýewa depicts a scene of a man and woman standing outside their yurt. The horse in the background is likely a representation of the Ahal-Tekke horse, cherished by the Turkmen for their beauty and ability to travel long distances. The predominant use of red recalls the traditional color scheme of Turkmen carpets which are also predominantly red.

Figure 44

"Our Home" (*"Biziñ öýümiz"*)

Annaguly Hojagulyýew (1947-) and Sulgun Hojagulyýewa (1949-)

20th century

Wool and cotton, gobelin flat weaving

50 X 80 cm

Museum of Fine Arts (Ashgabat)

Registry number: R-53 KEK-2883 (135 nf)

53

Figure 45
"Masters" (*"Ussatlar"*)
Amanmyrat Ataýew (1940-)
1985
Wool, gobelin flat weaving
170 X 100 cm
Museum of Fine Arts (Ashgabat)
Registry number: K-910 KEK-5915

Identity is always present in a craftmaker's aesthetic. Beyond the use of *göls* to symbolize one's tribal affiliation, carpet weavers also found subtle ways to honor their occupation through motifs. Designs inspired by aspects of the carpet-making process, including representations of weavers and tools such as the comb and spindle, are especially common in border patterns (Figure 47).

Gobelin artists also regarded traditional carpet-weaving as an important aspect of Turkmen cultural identity and used weavers as subjects for their artwork. The craftswomen in Amanmyrat Ataýew's "Masters" (Figure 45) are stitching a carpet in the *gurama* style, discussed above in relation to the checkered *gapylyk* (Figure 37). "Spinner" (Figure 46) by Sulgun Hojagulyýewa depicts a woman in national *keteni* dress and headwear as she prepares yarn with her spindle.

Figure 46

"Spinner" (*"Egriji"*)
Sulgun Hojagulyýewa (1949-)
Late 20th century
Wool and cotton, gobelin flat weaving
125 X 105 cm
Museum of Fine Arts (Ashgabat)
Registry number: AHS-134

Figure 47

This abstract representation of a carpet weaver from a traditional Turkmen weaving is distinguished by the comb designs to the left and right of the figure.

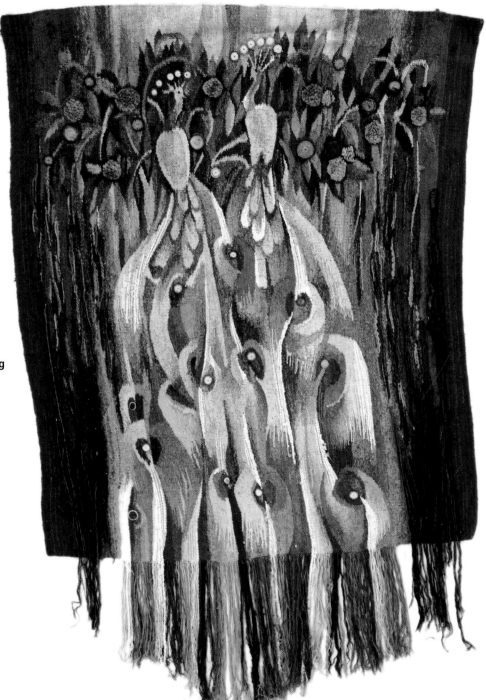

Figure 48

"Peacocks" ("*Tawus guşlar*")

Kakamyrat Baýlyýew (1949-1996)

1989

Wool and cotton, gobelin flat weaving

220 X 200 cm

Museum of Fine Arts (Ashgabat)

Registry number: AHS-136

Nature has inspired many traditional Turkmen designs including the *gushly göl*–bird (Figure 28), *pendi göl* –oasis (Figure 30), *gochack*—ram (Figure 36) and "tree of life" symbol (Figure 33, in the älem) discussed above.

While traditional nature imagery is necessarily abstract due to the geometric limitations of these designs, the subject matter in these gobelins is more easily recognized. "Peacocks" (Figure 48) by Kakamyrat Baýlyýew is a colorful and hypnotic representation of two peacocks. The use of the extended fringe to emphasize the feathers is an example of a production technique commonly used by Turkmen gobelin artists. "Autumn Poems" (Figure 49) by Annaguly Hojagulyýew and Sulgun Hojagulyýewa is a depiction of an apple tree blossoming before an array of fall colors.

Figure 49

"Autumn Poems" (*"Güýz goşgulary"*)

Annaguly Hojagulyýew (1947-) and Sulgun Hojagulyýewa (1949-)

20th century

Wool, gobelin flat weaving

175 X 96 cm

Museum of Fine Arts (Ashgabat)

Registry number: AHS-63

"Wedding" (Figure 50) by Amanmyrat Ataýew is the only painting featured in the exhibit. The Turkmen title, "Toý," specifically refers to the celebratory family gathering held in the event of weddings, births and holidays. At this toý, Turkmen ladies prepare the wedding feast as they await the arrival of the bride and groom. One woman cares for a newborn child while two men cook plov, a national dish, near a pair of automobiles. Celebrating a wedding, a newborn, or a holiday in such a fertile landscape surely represents and encourages the health and prosperity that can come through unions and new beginnings. With its incorporation of traditional and modern imagery in such an innovative and appealing form, this painting seems also to epitomize the celebration of Turkmen heritage in an aspiring and rapidly changing nation.

Figure 50

"Wedding" ("Toý")

Amanmyrat Ataýew (1940-)

1986

Tempera painting with alabaster and chalk priming mixture and bronze accents

70 X 50 cm

Museum of Fine Arts (Ashgabat)

Registry number: Ž-527

Figure 51

This monument to the arts (topped by stylized *dutar* stringed instruments), in a newly developed area of Ashgabat, testifies to contemporary Turkmenistan's dedication to the arts.

Bibliography

Abazov, Rafis. 2005. *Historical Dictionary of Turkmenistan*. Lanham, Maryland: Scarecrow.

Abbott, James. 1843. *Narrative of a Journey from Heraut to Khiva*. Moscow and St. Petersburgh. London: Allen.

Azadi, Siawosch. 1975. *Turkoman Carpets: and the ethnographic significance of their ornaments*. Fishguard, Wales: Crosby.

Baýryýewa, A. 2008. *Eňsi: Türkmeniň hala* çitrilen *rowayaty (Eňsi hakda kelam agyz söz) = Eňsi: Woven legends of Turkmen = Sokannie lezenq' Turkmen*. Aşgabat: Türkmenhaly Döwlet Paýdarlar Korporasiýasy.

Beckwith, Christopher I. 2009. *Empires of the Silk Road*. Princeton, New Jersey: Princeton University Press.

Beliaev, V. 1928. *Turkmenskaia muzyka*. Moskva: Gos. Izd-va Muzykal sektor.

Blackwell, Carole. 2001. *Tradition and Society in Turkmenistan: Gender, Oral Culture and Song*. Richmond: Curzon.

Christian, David. 2000. "Silk Roads or Steppe Roads? The Silk Roads in World History." *Journal of World History* 2(1):1-26.

Curtis, Glenn E. ed. 1996. *Turkmenistan: A Country Study*. Washington: GPO for the Library of Congress.

Edgar, Adrienne Lynn. 2003. "Emancipation of the Unveiled: Turkmen Women under Soviet Rule, 1924-29." *Russian Review* 62(1):132-49.

Edgar, Adrienne Lynn. 2004. *Tribal Nation: the Making of Soviet Turkmenistan*. Princeton: Princeton University Press.

Eiland, Murray L. 1973. *Oriental Rugs: A Comprehensive Guide*. Greenwich, Connecticut: New York Graphic Society.

Fedorov-Davydov, G. A. 1983. "Archaeological Research in Central Asia of the Muslim Period." *World Archaeology* 14(3):393-405.

Findley, Carter V. 2005. *The Turks in World History*. New York: Oxford University Press.

Fossum, David C. 2010. *The Ahal School : Turkmen Dutar and the Individual*. Middletown, Connecticut: Wesleyan.

Frumkin, Gregoire. 1970. *Archaeology in Central Asia*. Leiden: E.J. Brill.

Gantzhorn, Volkmar. 1998. *Oriental Carpets: Their Iconology and Iconography, from Earliest Times to the 18th Century*. Köln, New York: Taschen.

Golden, Peter B. 1992. *An Introduction to the History of the Turkic Peoples: Ethnogenesis and State-formation in Medieval and Early Modern Eurasia in the Middle East*. Wiesbaden: Otto Harrassowitz.

Grousset, René. 1970. *The Empire of the Steppes; A History of Central Asia*. New Brunswick, NJ: Rutgers University Press.

Herodotus., Strassler, Robert B., Purvis, Andrea L. 2007. *The Landmark Herodotus: the Histories*. New York: Pantheon Books

Irons, William. 1975. *The Yomut Turkmen: a Study of Social Organization among a Central Asian Turkic-speaking Population*. Ann Arbor: University of Michigan.

Krader, Lawrence. 1963. *Peoples of Central Asia*. Bloomington: Indiana University Publication.

Kurbanova, Dzhamilya. 2000. "The Singing Traditions of Turkmen Epic Poetry." 115-128 in: Karl Reichl (ed.) *The Oral Epic: Performance and Music*. Berlin: Verlag für Wissenschaft und Bildung.

Kuropatkin, A.N. 1899. *Zavoevanie Turkmenie: s ocherkom voennykh dieistvii v Srednei Azii s 1839 o 1876 g*. St. Petersburg: V. Berezovskii.

Kwanten, Luc. 1979. *Imperial Nomads: A History of Central Asia, 500-1500*. Philadelphia: University of Pennsylvania Press.

MacDonald, Brian W. 1997. *Tribal Rugs: Treasures of the Black Tent*. Woodbridge, Suffolk: Antique Collectors' Club.

Mair, Victor H. 2006. *Contact and Exchange in the Ancient World*. Honolulu: University of Hawai'i.

Martin, Terry. 2001. *The Affirmative Action Empire: Nations and Nationalism in the Soviet Union, 1923-1939*. Ithaca and London: Cornell University Press.

Masson, V. M. 1988. *Altyn-Depe*. Philadelphia: University Museum, University of Pennsylvania.

Masson, V. M., V. I. Sarianidi. 1972. *Central Asia: Turkmenia before the Achaemenids*. New York: Praeger.

Moshkova, V.G. 1980. "Tribal Göl in Turkoman Carpets." *Turkoman Studies I: Aspects of the Weaving and Decorative Arts of Central Asia*. Robert Pinner and Michael Franses, eds. London: Oguz Limited.

Moshkova, V. G., with A. S. Morosova, and M. F. Gavrilov. 1996. "Classification of Central Asian Rugs." Pp. 42-61 in: O›Bannon and Amanova-Olsen (1996).

Moshkova, V. G., with A. S. Morosova, and M. F. Gavrilov. 1996. "Weaving of the Salors." Pp. 179-192. in: O›Bannon and Amanova-Olsen (1996).

Moshkova, V. G., with A. S. Morosova, and M. F. Gavrilov.1996. "Weaving of the Yomuds." Pp. 229-25. in: O›Bannon and Amanova-Olsen (1996).

O›Bannon, George W. and Ovadan K. Amanova-Olsen (eds.) 1996. *Carpets of the People of Central Asia of the Late XIX and XX Centuries*. Tucson, AZ: George O'Bannon.

Opie, James.1998. *Tribal Rugs: A Complete Guide to Nomadic and Village Carpets*. Boston: Bulfinch.

Ponomaryov, O. 1980. "The Motifs of Turkmoman Carpets-Salor, Tekke, and Saryk."Turkoman Studies I: Aspects of the weaving and decorative arts of Central Asia. Robert Pinner and Michael Franses, eds. London: Oguz Limited.

Pugachenkova, Galina Anatolevna. 1956. *Ocherki po istorii iskusstva Turkmenistana*. Askhabad: Turkmengosizdat.

Saray, Mehmet. 1989. *The Turkmens in the Age of Imperialism: a Study of the Turkmen People and Their Incorporation into the Russian Empire*. Ankara: Turkish Historical Society Printing House.

Sarianidi, V.I. 2011. *Historical and Cultural Sites of Turkmenistan*. Aşgabat: Turkmen döwlet neşirýat gullugy.

Schletzer, Dieter and Reinhold Schletzer. 1984. Old Silver Jewellery of the Turkoman: an essay on symbols in the culture of Inner Asian nomads. Berlin: Reimer.

Semenov-Tian-Shanskii.,Veniamin Petrovich.1899-1914. *Rossiia; polnoe geograficheskoe opisanie nashego otechestva*. St. Petersburg: Izd. A.F. Devriena.(11 v.)

Starr, Frederick S. 2009. "Rediscovering Central Asia." *The Wilson Quarterly* 33(3):33-43.

Stone, Peter F. 2007. *Tribal & Village Rugs: The Definitive Guide to Design, Pattern & Motif*. New York: Thames & Hudson.

Suny, Ronald Grigor. 1993. *The Revenge of the Past: Nationalism, Revolution and the Collapse of the Soviet Union*. Stanford, CA: Stanford University Press.

Brown, John Porter (editor & translator). 1849-1850. "Et-Tabary's conquest of Persia by the Arabs." *Journal of the American Oriental Society* v. 1 (1849) p. [437-505; v. 2 (1850) p. [209]-234.

Tsareva, Elena.1984. *Rugs & Carpets from Central Asia: the Russian Collections*. Leningrad: Aurora Art Publishers.

Tsareva, Elena. 2011. Turkmen Carpets: Masterpieces of Steppe Art, from 16th to 19th Centuries; the Hoffmeister Collection. Stuttgart: Arnoldsche.

[TMTM] Türkmenistanyn Medeniýet we Teleradioýaýlymlar Ministrligi
2009 *Türkmenistanyn muzeýleri = Museums of Turkmenistan = Muzei Turkmenistana*. Ashgabat: Türkmenistanyn Medeniýet we Teleradioýaýlymlar Ministrligi.

[TNC] Turkmen National Conservatory. n.d. "Turkmen National Conservatory." [Informational brochure, distributed at Turkmen National Conservatory, Ashgabat, in 2011.]

Vambery,Armin. 1867. *Puteshestvie po Srednei Azii*. Moskva: Izd. A.I. Mamontova.

Zeranska-Kominek, Slawomira. 1990. "The Classification of Repertoire in Turkmen Traditional Music." *Asian Music* 21(2):91-108.

Żerańska-Kominek, Sławomira, and Arnold Lebeuf. 1997. *The Tale of Crazy Harman: the Musician and the Concept of Music in the Türkmen Epic Tale, Harman Däli*. Warsaw: Academic Publications Dialog.

Photo Credits

Photographs for the publication have been provided by Smithsonian researchers Jasper Waugh-Quasebarth (Figures 2, 5, 6, 8, 9, 18, 20, 21, 24-56; Watermarks pp. 35, 36-37; Cover Images 1,5,6,7 from left), William Bradford Smith (Figures 10,11,23,25; Cover Images 2,3,4 from left) and Trevor Merrion (Figure 4; Watermark pp. 15); The Ministry of Culture of Turkmenistan (Figures 1,3,12-15,19, 22; Watermarks pp. 16-19, 22, 24-26, 30) and the National Parlimentary Library of Georgia (Figures 16,17; Cover Watermarks). Map of Turkmenistan (Figure 7) by Marcia Bakry.

Photographs of museum objects and settings were taken with permission of the respective museums and published courtesy of the Ministry of Culture of Turkmenistan.

Archival printed images watermarks (background images) on the covers were photographed by William Bradford Smith at the National Parliamentary Library of Georgia. *Front cover:* Print, "Priem u Turkmenskikh iachalnikov na berego kaspiiskago mora" ["Reception for Turkmen Chiefs on the Shore of the Caspian Sea"], from: *Puteshestvie po Srednei Azii* by Armin Vambery (1867, Moskva: Izd. A.I. Mamontova). *Back cover:* Turkmen, print from pencil drawing, "Turkmeny, Sarty" from: *Sredi znojnych pustyn' i sirokich stepej narody Turkestana* by Evgenij E. Sno (1904, St. Petersburg: Popov).

Endpapers: Monochrome traced outline of central panel patterns from Floor Carpet shown in Figure 30.

Acknowledgments

The authors thank the Ministry of Culture of Turkmenistan, and the Directors and staff of the many Museums in Turkmenistan we visited; especially the two museums who loaned to this exhibition, the Main National Museum of Turkmenistan and the Museum of Fine Arts. We also thank Ambassador Robert Patterson and his staff at the Embassy of the U.S.A. in Ashgabat (especially William Stevens, Courtney Doggart, and Maya Meredova), and Ambassador Meret Orazov and his staff at the Embassy of Turkmenistan in Washington. Within the Smithsonian, many helped with this project, especially the staff of the Department of Anthropology (Dr. Mary Jo Arnoldi, Chair), the Smithsonian Institution Libraries (Dr. Nancy Gwinn, Director; Dr. Margaret Dittemore, Anthropology Librarian); and the Office of Policy and Analysis (Dr. Carole Neves, Director). We appreciate the hospitality and access to the libraries of the National Parliamentary Library of Georgia, and the library of the Georgian State Museum of Theatre, Music, & Cinema (both in Tbilisi, Georgia). We are grateful for the professionalism and the quality of exhibition work by all our colleagues at Meridian International Center, especially Dr. Curtis Sandberg, Terry Harvey, and Lindsay Amini.

The generous support of Chevron has made the Turkmenistan Culture Days in Washington and this publication possible; our sincere thanks go to Diana Sedney of Chevron's Washington office, and to Douglas Uchikura of Chevron Nebitgaz B.V. Turkmenistan, and their staffs.

The authors serve as researchers in the Smithsonian's Asian Cultural History Program (ACHP), where Paul M. Taylor also serves as Director; we thank all our ACHP colleagues for their help in this cooperative work with Turkmenistan's museums, especially Jared Koller and Robert Pontsioen.

Figure 52

An equestrian statue atop a fountain in Ashgabat honoring Oguz Khan, legendary progenitor of the Turkmen people, and his six sons.

Figure 53

Avenues lined with marble apartment buildings are a common feature in modern Ashgabat.

67

Figure 54

A statue of a Turkmen horseman looks on to the golden dome of the Palace of the President in Ashgabat.

68

Figure 55

In the weeks before the October 2011 celebration of Turkmenistan's twentieth anniversary of independence, Ahal-Tekke horsemen practice for the anniversary parade in front of the Presidential Palace in Ashgabat.

Figure 56

As part of preparations for the twentieth anniversary celebrations, workers upgrade a street in downtown Ashgabat, flanked by Turkmenistan's Supreme Court, its Central Bank, The Ministry of Culture, and The International Ahal-Tekke Horse Breeders Association.